3/12

Let's Throw a Valentine's Day Party!

Rachel Lynette

PowerKiDS press

New York

For Dr. Adam

Published in 2012 by The Rosen Publishing Group, Inc.
29 East 21st Street, New York, NY 10010

First Edition

Editor: Joanne Randolph
Layout Design: Greg Tucker

Photo Credits: Cover (main, inset), pp. 4–5, 9, 14 (left), 15, 18, 19 Shutterstock.com; p. 6 Hulton Archive/Getty Images; p. 7 Bob Thomas/Popperfoto/Getty Images; pp. 8, 11 Tetra Images/Getty Images; p. 10 © www.iStockphoto.com/Tamás Dernovics; p. 12 Katy McDonnell/Digital Vision/Thinkstock; p. 13 Comstock Images/Getty Images; p. 14 (right) David Johnston/Getty Images; p. 16 Jean Maurice/Getty Images; p. 17 Friedrich Strauss/Getty Images; p. 22 Jupiterimages/Brand X Pictures/Thinkstock.

Library of Congress Cataloging-in-Publication Data

Lynette, Rachel.
 Let's throw a Valentine's Day party! / by Rachel Lynette. — 1st ed.
    p. cm. — (Holiday parties)
 Includes index.
 ISBN 978-1-4488-2570-7 (library binding) — ISBN 978-1-4488-2729-9 (pbk.) — ISBN 978-1-4488-2730-5 (6-pack)
 1. Valentine decorations—Juvenile literature. 2. Valentine's Day cooking—Juvenile literature. 3. Entertaining—Juvenile literature. 4. Children's parties—Juvenile literature. I. Title.
 TT900.V34L96 2012
 793.2′2—dc22
                                          2010030250
Manufactured in the United States of America

CPSIA Compliance Information: Batch #WW11PK: For Further Information contact Rosen Publishing, New York, New York at 1-800-237-9932

Contents

Happy Valentine's Day!

Have you ever received a special valentine? Giving valentines to your family and friends is an important part of Valentine's Day. People often give cards, candy, flowers, and other gifts to one another. Many people also throw parties on Valentine's Day.

This book will give you ideas about how to throw a Valentine's Day party that your friends will love! There are tips for making fun **decorations** and yummy treats. There are also ideas for making your own valentines and valentine holders. Of course, no party would be complete without games either! What are you waiting for? Let's start planning!

Making valentines is fun. It shows the people you love that you care about them, too!

No one knows exactly how Valentine's Day began. However, there is a story about a **bishop** named Valentine who lived in Rome around AD 270. At that time, the **emperor**, Claudius II, passed a law that said that **soldiers** could not get married.

Thinking the law unfair, Valentine secretly married young couples. When he was

Here Saint Valentine is being brought to prison. Some people thought Valentine had the power to make sick people better.

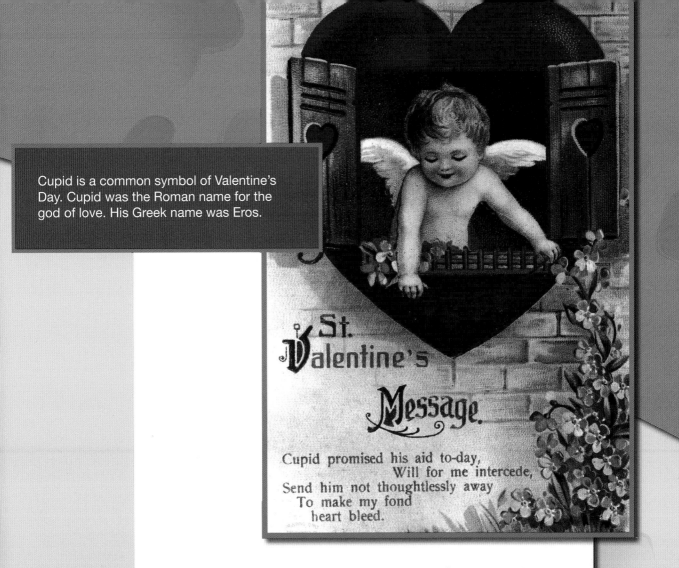

Cupid is a common symbol of Valentine's Day. Cupid was the Roman name for the god of love. His Greek name was Eros.

St. Valentine's Message.

Cupid promised his aid to-day,
Will for me intercede,
Send him not thoughtlessly away
To make my fond
heart bleed.

caught, he was put in **prison** to wait for **execution**. While there, he formed a friendship with the prison guard's daughter. Before he was executed, he wrote a good-bye note to her and signed it "From your Valentine." Years later, February 14 was made a **feast day** to honor Saint Valentine.

Party Planning

Planning a party is not hard if you start early. Start planning your party in the middle of January. Begin by making a list of the people you would like to invite.

You will also need to make a list of all the things you will need for your party. Think

If you plan on making your own invitations, be sure to include the supplies you will need to make them on your shopping list.

Making a list of what you want to do or buy for your party will help you remember everything.

about what kind of decorations you would like to have. You will also want to plan what kind of food you want to serve. Finally, you will want to think about what your guests will do at your party. What games will you play? Will your guests do a craft project?

Be Mine, Valentine!

In the **Middle Ages** people in Europe made valentines with lace, ribbons, feathers, and pressed flowers. The **custom** spread to the American **colonies**. It was not until the 1840s that people could buy Valentine's Day cards.

Try This!

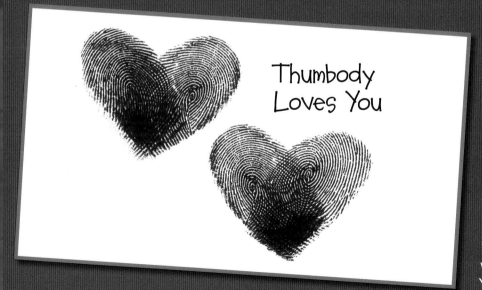

Thumbody Loves You

To make a fun valentine, you just need construction paper, scissors, a red stamp pad, and your thumbs! Cut the construction paper into a 5-inch (13 cm) square. Press your thumb onto the stamp pad and make a heart shape on the paper with your thumbprints. Then write "Thumbody Loves You" on the card!

You can glue different-sized heart cutouts or doilies together to make a pretty valentine. It can be a fun project to do with a parent or a friend, too!

Although millions of valentines are now sold every year, it is still fun to make them yourself. Use colors like red, pink, purple, and white. You can use heart cutouts, **doilies**, lace, and glitter to decorate your cards. Do not forget to write a valentine greeting such as, "Be Mine" or "Happy Valentine's Day." Your friends and family members will be happy to get one of your special valentines!

Let's Decorate!

It is fun to make Valentine's Day decorations. Decorate the walls with large heart cutouts. You can leave your cutouts plain or decorate them with crayons and glitter. You might want to hang smaller cutouts from the ceiling, too. Just cut out three or four hearts about the size of salad plates. Then tape them to a piece of string.

Try This!

1. To make a paper chain, use strips of red, purple, pink, and white construction paper.
2. Tape the ends of the first strip together to make a ring shape.
3. Then put the next strip through the hole in the first one. Tape the ends together to make a second ring.
4. Keep going until your chain is the size you want. Have fun!

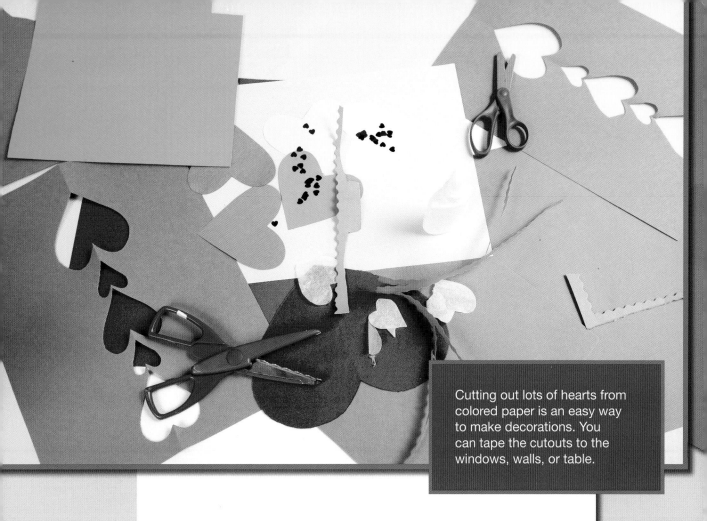

Cutting out lots of hearts from colored paper is an easy way to make decorations. You can tape the cutouts to the windows, walls, or table.

Paper chains are also fun to make. You can follow the steps in the box to the left to find out how to make your own. Do not forget about balloons. You can hang them in a group from the ceiling. You can also get **helium** balloons and tie them to the chairs.

Party Treats

What will you serve your guests at your party? Heart-shaped cookies are easy to make. Just use a heart-shaped cookie cutter. You could also have pink and red jelly beans, chocolate kisses, or cupcakes with pink frosting.

You can make heart-shaped brownies (above) and sugar cookies (right) with the same cookie cutters. Have fun decorating the cookies with colored sugar or frosting!

Cupcakes with white frosting can be dusted with pink or red sugar. You can also use heart-shaped candy sprinkles.

How about a heart-shaped pizza? Just make the dough into a heart shape instead of a circle. After you put the sauce and cheese on, decorate your heart pizza with whatever toppings you like.

Do not forget to offer guests something to drink, such as pink lemonade or a berry-flavored punch. Look for a heart-shaped ice-cube tray when you shop for supplies. Use it to make special heart-shaped ice cubes for your punch!

Make your table **festive** by decorating it in Valentine's Day colors. How about using a red tablecloth with pink napkins? You can make fun napkin rings by twisting pink, red, and white pipe cleaners into a circle. Next, make heart-shaped place mats from white paper and leave crayons and stickers at each place. Your guests will have fun decorating their own place mats. You could have them decorate their own plates and cups, too!

Putting plates of different sizes and patterns on top of each other, as shown here, can make your table look extra nice. Red and pink balloons are a fun table decoration, too!

You can tie your napkins into heart shapes like the ones here. Use plastic cups and let your guests paint them, too!

Make place cards for your guests by writing their names on heart cutouts. You can decorate your place cards with candy conversation hearts. If you use glue, just make sure your guests do not try to eat them!

Everyone loves to play games at a party! Try this fun game. Give each player a plate full of jelly beans, a paper cup, and a pair of chopsticks. Set a timer for 2 minutes. The players must use the chopsticks to get the jelly beans into their cups. Whoever gets the most jelly beans in her cup, wins!

After your guests use their chopsticks to put jelly beans into their cups, they can eat the jelly beans!

Cut out the hearts for your heart hunt a few days before the party. You can hide them the morning before your guests arrive.

You can also have a heart hunt. Use construction paper to cut a different-color heart for each guest. Cut each heart into four pieces. Hide all the pieces before the party. To play, each guest must find all four pieces of his color and then put the heart together!

Make a Valentine Holder

Your guests will have fun making their own valentine holders.

What you need:

Paper plates
Stapler
Scissors
Glue
Markers or crayons
Hole punch
Ribbon
Decorating materials, such as glitter, sequins, ribbon, yarn, lace, stickers, doilies, and heart cutouts

What you do:

1

Give each guest two paper plates. Have everyone cut one of the paper plates in half.

2

Put the eating sides of the half plate and the whole plate together to make a pocket. Staple around the edges.

3

To make heart cutouts, have everyone fold a piece of colored paper in half. Next draw half a heart shape on the paper, as shown. Cut out the shape and unfold your hearts!

Have your guests make their valentine holders as soon as they arrive at your party. Then the glue will have time to dry before you pass out valentines at the end.

4

Write your name or a Valentine's greeting on the front of the pocket and decorate it.

5

Use the hole punch to make two holes at the top of your holder. Thread the ribbon through the holes and tie it to make a carrier.

Special Delivery

It is fun to give valentines at a Valentine's Day party. At the end of your party, have your guests put out their valentine holders. Then everyone can deliver their special valentines. You might want to play some lively music while people are delivering their cards.

> Guests will enjoy opening the valentines they receive at your party. If time is running out, though, they can bring them home to open.

Cleaning up after your party can be a big job. You might want to ask one or two of your friends to stay late and help. Now that you have had your first Valentine's Day party, you have some decorations to save for next year!

Glossary

bishop (BIH-shep) A leader in a church, such as the Roman Catholic Church.

colonies (KAH-luh-neez) New places where people move that are still ruled by the leaders of the countries from which they came.

custom (KUS-tum) A practice common to many people in a place or a social class.

decorations (deh-kuh-RAY-shunz) Objects that make things prettier.

doilies (DOY-leez) Lacy mats made from paper or cloth.

emperor (EM-per-er) The ruler of an empire or of several countries.

execution (ek-suh-KYOO-shun) The act of putting someone to death.

feast day (FEEST DAY) A day that honors a saint.

festive (FES-tiv) Fun, or ready for a party.

helium (HEE-lee-um) A light, colorless gas.

Middle Ages (MIH-dul AY-jez) The period in European history from about AD 500 to about 1450.

prison (PRIH-zun) A place where people who break laws are held.

soldiers (SOHL-jurz) People who are in an army.

Index

Web Sites

Due to the changing nature of Internet links, PowerKids Press has developed an online list of Web sites related to the subject of this book. This site is updated regularly. Please use this link to access the list: www.powerkidslinks.com/hp/valen/